WALKS IN THE

Land of Oak and Iron

by **Tim Deveaux**

Typeset in Minion Pro

Editing, design and publishing by Printmeit.com Ltd
www.printmeit.com

ISBN: 978-1-5272-4230-2

Contents

Introduction

This book describes 11 walks in the area designated, The Land of Oak and Iron. The walks attempt to pass many of the sites that the Land of Oak and Iron wish to highlight. Not all of these sites are covered in this book. Several sites are covered in my first book, Walks in the Derwent Valley. Those walks are:

Walk 1 Derwenthaugh Park
Walk 2 Gibside
Walk 4 Chopwell Woods
Walk 5 Ebchester and Derwentcote Steel Furnace
Walk 7 Shotley Bridge and Hownsgill Viaduct
Walk 8 Derwent Gorge and Muggleswick Woods

The routes in this book vary from 4.5 to 9 miles, but are mostly of moderate difficulty based on a fairly fit 65 year old!!

Part of the Derwent valley is in an area of outstanding natural beauty and there are some stunning views of the whole valley and some unexpected features throughout the walks.

The walks include descriptions of some of the places visited in each walk. I hope this helps to enhance the walks even more than the beautiful places you will see. I have also included a wide range of refreshment hostelries where you may want to have a well earned break! Many are coffee and tea stops but there are some with stronger tipples. I tend to go for either a coffee and bacon sandwich or a pint of real ale!

Some walks near the confluence of the Derwent and the Tyne can be quite busy, but some are very tranquil and you may only see sheep and other 'wildlife' during your walking experience.

I have three aims in writing my walking books:
1. To keep public footpaths open and in good condition.
2. To keep the countryside free of litter.
3. For those who walk the routes to enjoy the beautiful countryside!

I would encourage all walkers to pick up litter on your walk and take home and put it in your bin.

Wildlife and landscape
These walks give you an opportunity to appreciate the variety of landscapes in the valley. Most are woodland walks or through open fields and some are close to a Rivers Tyne or Derwent.

The valley is also home to a large number of Red Kites. These impressive birds can be seen every day in the skies above Rowlands Gill and the Derwent Walk. You may here their screech call before you see them but once you do you will be greatly impressed by their size and beauty.

There are a wide range of habitats in the valley - woodlands, meadows, wetlands, riverside and reclaimed industrial sites.

In the woodlands you will see wood anemones and celandines in spring. Butterflies such as the common blue and meadow brown can be seen in the meadows. There are many birds including green woodpecker, great spotted woodpecker, nuthatch and bullfinch, mistle thrush and song thrush. There are several hunting birds including sparrowhawk. You may also see fox, badger and roe deer. On and in the River Derwent itself you may see kingfisher, dipper and otter.

Maps and rights of way
Most walks follow public rights of way footpaths and bridle ways with some following roads, some quiet and some with a modest amount of traffic. These pathways are signposted, mostly, when leaving a road. There are some permissive paths. Please use the paths and grass verges where indicated.

Most walks are circular (two are point to point) and are provided with an approximate distance, an assessment of difficulty, estimated time and starting point which is always the end point, if a circular walk. A map of each walk is also provided to guide you through the walk in addition to the description of the route. It is advisable that you take an ordnance survey map with you to double check your route in case you go wrong. I hope this is unlikely!!!! I used the OS explorer series maps for the routes.

Clothing and footwear

Wear sturdy shoes but preferably walking shoes or boots. It can be muddy at certain times of year, so be prepared. Gaiters will be useful for some walks and warm comfortable socks will make the experience much more pleasurable. Always take a waterproof top and if you feel it necessary, waterproof trousers. The British weather is notoriously fickle!

Safety

Some walks are near the river so be very careful when you get close to the riverbank. Non slip shoes or boots are useful for most walks. If you are an experienced walker your clothing will cope with most scenarios.

Respect for the countryside

Leave the countryside how you find it. Close gates where they are closed, leave them open if they are open. Take litter home. Keep to the route. You will come across cattle, sheep and horse. Always treat them with respect and caution. Some can be a little feisty! If you have a dog with you, always keep it under control and on a lead when near livestock.

Walk 1: Newburn Bridge, Ryton Willows, Clara Vale, and Ryton

Distance	6.2 miles
Time	2.5 hours
Difficulty	Easy
Parking	North of the Newburn Bridge near the Boathouse Pub, Newburn
Public Transport	13, 22, 22X, 71

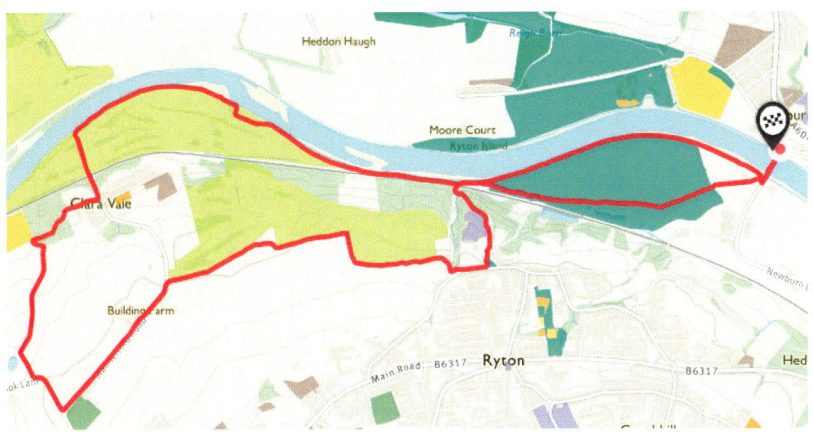

Begin at the Boathouse pub next to Newburn Bridge. Walk to the bridge and cross it and at the south side turn right to the path alongside the river. Follow this path for about 2.3 miles up river passing Ryton Willows and Ryton Golf Course. When you get to the western end of the Golf Course there is a cycle signpost for Clara Vale and Crawcrook.

Take this left turn to a gate, crossing the railway track with caution. Follow the road up hill and at the road junction turn right past a terrace of houses called East View and between the terraces of Edington Gardens. The track widens but you soon come to the entrance of the Clara Vale Nature Reserve. Go through the entrance gate, you can bear left or right to walk through the reserve. Both take you to the western exit of the reserve. Going through the exit gate and turn left past a small area parking area. Carry on for about 40 yards and turn right at a public footpath sign.

Follow the footpath signs for about quarter of a mile to a road. Turn left at the road and in about 200 yards turn left again into Stannerford road. Follow this road for about quarter of a mile past bungalows and a farm. Soon after another few bungalows there is a public footpath sign to your right.

Cross the road and follow this path into the golf course. Beware of golf balls for the next half a mile! Follow the public footpath through the golf course till you come to a large public footpath signpost just before a single story stone building. Turn right through the green keepers buildings to follow a lane alongside the golf course until you come to a tarmaced road. Follow this road to your right and in front of you is the Ryton Pinfold.

Here, turn left along the road till you come to Ryton village green. Turn left towards the entrance to the Holy Cross Church. Just before this, turn right and immediately left to a public footpath through the trees. Follow the path down to a crossing over the railway.

Cross the railway with caution and turn right along the path by the river past a house and bear right to a gate. Go through the gate and into Ryton Willows onto a path which follows the railway line. Soon it veers left away from it towards the river.

At the eastern end of the Willows go through the gate and into an enclosed path. At the end of this path cross the field ahead, ignoring the tarmaced roads and paths. This takes you to the south end of Newburn Bridge. Cross the bridge back to the parking area.

Refreshments
The Boathouse, Newburn, NE15 8NL Tel.0191 267 7308.

Battle of Newburn Ford
An important battle in English History took place here in 1640. The battle was part of a revolt by the Scots against King Charles 1 and his introduction of a new prayer book led eventually to the English Civil War.

On 28 August 1640 the English and the Scots faced each other here across the Tyne. A hastily assembled English force of about 3,500 reluctantly stood against as many as 22,500 Scots. The Scots occupying the higher ground north of the river not only had a force which was better fed, drilled and motivated but had five times as many cannons. The Scottish commander, General Alexander Leslie, wanted to capture a wealthy Newcastle and its surrounding coalfields to exert pressure on the King. He decided to cross the Tyne to attack the city from its weaker southern side. Newburn was the first crossing place west of Newcastle.

The English commander, Lord Conway, although ordered to fight, realised his position was hopeless.

Arriving at Stella in the evening on 27 August he drew out the English force on Stella Haugh. Local troops had been busy building two defensive earthworks into which Conway placed 400 musketeers and 4 cannons. On the morning of the 28th the 2 armies faced each other. Conway found an ally in the River Tyne as the river could only be crossed between 2 and 3 o'clock in the afternoon. Fighting began at midday when an English musketeer shot at and wounded a Scottish Officer watering his horse. The Scottish Cavalry charged across the river but were driven back by gunfire. Heavy bombardment began from both sides. The Scottish cavalry tried to cross the river for a second time and were driven back by a courageous English cavalry led by Commissary Henry Wilmot. The Scottish cavalry tried for a third time to cross the river and this time were successful.

The English quickly retreated in confusion and as a result there were few casualties. The infantry fled towards Newcastle but the cavalry headed in the opposite direction to higher ground where some officers and Wilmot were captured. Following the battle, the Scots occupied Newcastle and the surrounding coalfields with the civilian population fleeing in fear. King Charles 1 was forced to recall Parliament to obtain the money needed to buy the Scots off. Parliament voted for the necessary £200,000 but refused to be dissolved, bringing it into conflict with the king and leading to the English Civil War which broke out two years later.

River Tyne

Despite being 17 miles from the sea the River Tyne is still tidal at Ryton and the water level rises and falls dramatically during the day. The river did not look the way it does today. Historically it would have flowed onto the willows during high tide and in times of flood. However, in the 19th century it was dredged and the slag from Stanner Steel works at Newburn was deposited on both sides of the river to consolidate the bank sides reducing flooding of the surrounding areas.

From the 14th till the mid 20th century people used to cross the river at Ryton via ferry and the wooden remains of the jetty on the Newcastle side can still be seen today.

Clara Vale

In 1889 the two shafts of the Clara Vale pit were sunk on the site by the Stella Coal company. By 1897 the pit was producing 180,000 tons of coal a year and at its height employed nearly a thousand men. Almost all of the village community was involved in some way. The pit was closed in 1966 for economic reasons. The site of the pit reverted back to nature and villagers successfully campaigned to protect it. In 1986 it became a nature reserve managed by the Clara Vale Conservation group. Since 1986 ponds have been created, hedges planted and hides built.

Ryton Pinfold

An enclosure called a pinfold dating back to the 12th century was use to enclose stray animals till the owner paid a fine. The pinfold had a stream flowing through it to water the animals.

Ryton

Ryton's location as the lowest fordable point on the Tyne gave rise to its turbulent past. The village whose name means 'settlement by the river' was attacked several times by the Scots including William Wallace who burned it to the ground in 1297.

The Holy Cross church has a spire which is the only one of its type in the North of England. The Church modernised in the 18th and 19th century dates back as far as 1220 although there is a reference to an earlier church in 1112. In the Churchyard there is a large mound thought to be a prehistoric burial site, but now known to be a motte of an early mediaeval castle. The church was probably built inside the walls of the castle. The village green used to have stocks, and fairs were held twice a year until they were banned in 1866 because of drunkenness, noise and fighting. The Market Cross was erected in 1795 and renewed in 1951 probably replacing an earlier medieval structure. In the 18th century several large houses were built by wealthy businessmen and engineers. The White House once house the 'Penny Savings Bank', probably the first in the Country. Elvaston Hall was the home of Sir Charles Parsons. Parsons invented the steam turbine generator which made possible the generation of electricity for our modern lighting and heating. Parsons also developed steam turbine engines for ships and tested a model of the ship, Turbinia, on a pond in his garden. The success of the Turbinia gave a great boost to shipbuilding on the Tyne.

Ryton Willows

In Edwardian times, the main part of the Willows was the site of a mini fairground with roundabouts, 'shuggy boats' and a café. There were also boats to hire on the ponds. Now it is nature reserve and the ponds are Sites of Special Scientific Interest because they have a very rich flora and fauna.

Walk 2: The Spetchells, Prudhoe Castle and Cherryburn

Distance	6 miles
Time	2.5 hours
Difficulty	Moderate
Parking	Tyne Riverside Country Park, Low Prudhoe
Public Transport	Trains, Buses 10B and 10X

Start at the Tyne Riverside Country Park car park. Head to the riverside pathway and turn right along the path alongside the river and under the 'Skinny road bridge' heading downstream for about 1½ miles passing the white soil hills of the Spetchells on your right along the way.

Follow the riverside path passing by two houses, over a cattle grid, through a field, along a wide path, walking away from the river and past a junction coming to the houses at Hagg Bank. Pass in front of them and cross the bridge over the railway line. About 10 yards past the bridge turn right at a public footpath sign and into woodland. Follow the obvious path till you come to a fence (of a pumping station) and walk alongside it with it on your right until you come to an access track.

Turn left along the track and in about 100 yards turn right along a woodland path until you come to a gate, up some steps to a main road. Cross the road to another gate and a signposted wide path. Follow this path around the edge of a field and as you come to an incline in the path bear left up the incline to another road. Cross the road to the signposted path to Prudhoe Castle 1 mile.

You are now walking through Castlefields Wood. Follow the obvious wide path keeping left, eventually crossing a wooden bridge which is about ¾ way through the woods. Continue on the path and just past a caravan/car storage area on your right bear left uphill and at a fork in the path follow the permissive path sign steeply uphill eventually coming to some steps which you climb. At the top bear right to a tarmaced path.

You will see Prudhoe castle in the distance. Follow this until you come to the castle on your right. Follow the road past the castle till you come to a main road. Cross it heading straight ahead into Castle View.

Follow this road and into an enclosed path with gardens on your left and fields to your right. At the end of this path turn left up the lane, and in about 30 yards, turn right and follow this estate road, past a school, for about ¼ of a mile.

At the end of the road pass through the fence opening and turn right down a tarmaced road and then immediately left to a gate then onto the main road. Cross the road and with the factory to your right and bear left to a restricted byway sign to Eltringham house ½ mile. When you come to a 4 way road/path junction turn left uphill and follow this for about 300 yards and on your left is the entrance to Cherryburn.

Retrace your steps back to the main road next to the factory. As you approach the factory take the small footpath next to the factory fence before you get to the main road. At the end of the fence turn left at a public footpath sign into the woods. Follow the left hand track for about ¼ mile coming to a sunken path soon and when you come to a gate this leads to a crossing of the railway line. Cross the railway line and take the obvious path back to the Tyne Riverside car park where you started.

Refreshments

Tyne Riverside Cafe, Riverside Country Park Station Road, Prudhoe NE42 6NP
Tel. 01661 832911.

The Spetchells

The Spetchells are chalk waste heaps from the former ICI chemical factory. The factory made fertilizer for the 'Dig for victory' campaign but closed in 1967. The name comes from old maps that refer to this area of land as the 'spetchells'.

Although the heaps are not natural, they now provide Northumberland's largest area of chalk grassland habitat. The wide range of flowers attracts many species of common and, occasionally, rare butterflies. The area is noted for its population of Dingy Skipper Butterflies. Trees have grown up, such as Ash, Swedish Whitebeam, False Acacia and gorse is widespread.

Prudhoe Castle

The 12th Century stronghold of the D'Umfravilles and Percys. It has turbulent past and is famous for being the only castle in the north never to have been taken by the Scots.

It has a moat, a fine gateway and a Georgian Manor house built on the site of medieval buildings. The chapel above the gateway contains the earliest know oriel window in England. The castle was built upon a natural mound with steep natural scarps on the north and west sides. It was divided into Inner and Outer Wards.

It has bridge with a rounded arch on one side and a pointed arch on the other.
The two storey manor house was constructed in the early nineteenth century straddling the original divide between Inner and Outer Wards.

Cherryburn

This small farmhouse was the birthplace of Thomas Bewick, Northumberland's greatest artist, wood engraver and naturalist, he revolutionised print art in Georgian England. The building is now a National Trust museum where you can learn all about his life and see many of his artworks, set in a beautiful garden perfect for exploring with younger family members.

The Cottage has been furnished with items which would have been common at the time and the Farmhouse possesses a large collection of Bewick's publications, original engravings and printing equipment.

Thomas Bewick was born in the cottage in August 1753. He grew up there until the age of 14 when he moved to Newcastle upon Tyne to become an engraving apprentice with the Beilby family.

Walk 3: Wylam to Winlaton Mill (Tyne to Derwent)

Distance	9 miles
Time	3.5/4 hours
Difficulty	Moderate
Parking	Wylam Village car park or Wylam station car park
Public Transport	Trains to Wylam station or 686, X84

Walk across Wylam bridge if parked on the north village car park or walk away from Wylam bridge on the path on the left hand side of the road if parked in the station car park.

Walk up the road towards Crawcrook and turn right towards Daniel Farm and in about 100 metres turn left across a small stream to a stile. Cross it to a field and head uphill to the right of a woodland to another stile. Head to the left of the house ahead onto a track which runs by Bradley Gardens.

Ignore the track to the left opposite the house and continue on the track to follow the public footpath sign to the left to a narrow path through the trees with the Bradley pond on your right. Keep left on the high path. Eventually you come an enclosed path which you follow towards the road and alongside it till you come to some steps and at the top emerging onto the road. Cross the road to a bus stop and a path up between the houses and into a housing estate.

When you get to the road turn left and in 100 metres or so turn right into Horsley Avenue. Head up to the top of the road where the road forks and go straight ahead to a path between the houses into an enclosed path to a stile. Turn left uphill to a gate (ignore the first gate on the right) and then do a U turn to the path with the fence on your right. This takes you to the road.

Cross the road and turn left to walk on the grass verge for about 200 metres and turn right up hill into the trees with the fence on your left. At the top of this short hill is a gate (you may have to climb over a barrier here). Go through it and bear right up the hill keeping to the left of gorse and other shrubs till you come to a wide track. Turn right uphill and in about 50 metres turn right to a stile. Cross over the stile and turn left around the edge of the field. In about 400 metres at the top right corner of the field turn left uphill into a wood with the hedge on your left.

In about 20 metres turn right along a wide track. Follow this path for about 300 metres and ignore the first pubic footpath sign to the left and at the second sign turn left to a narrow path. After about 40 metres turn right to a stone stile. Cross it and the field to a road. Cross the road and head to the road opposite (Kyo Lane) and along that for about 300 metres. Turn left at the fingerpost.

Cross the stile and keeping the hedge to your right to a stile. Then bear diagonally right across the field to a gap in the fence to the right of the gate. Turn right along the road till you get to Coalburns and then turn left opposite the end of Coalburns cottages and through several stiles and fields till you come to the last field before a road. After crossing the stile to this last field bear right to an opening in the trees to cross a stream and follow the line of the trees and burn till you come to a stile and onto the road. Cross the road to another stile and then follow the burn which is to your left over several stiles. After about half a mile the track bears right up hill through the trees and then emerges at a field. Cross the field diagonally left to a stile in the hedge and head straight up to a gate which emerges onto a road. Turn left through Barlow till you get to South Farm (at the end of the path on the left hand side of the road).

Turn right into the farm yard then immediately right onto a farm track. Follow this for about half a mile till you get to a road. Turn right and follow this road for another half a mile. Turn left at two fingerposts and take the left hand one. Across a couple of stiles to an enclosed path across another stile onto the obvious path and follow this to the road at Thornley Lane (ignore a path under a stone bridge).

Cross the road heading down a drive to two houses and go between them to the path to the side of a field and follow this turning left down to an enclosed path to the main road. Cross the road to the signed path and follow the board walk to another path passing behind the Thornley Woodland Centre.

This path takes you through the woods to a field and a path to the side of that field. At the end of the field is a gate to an enclosed path. At the bottom is another gate taking you to another one. Turn right onto the Derwent walk and turn left along the track to the Land of Oak and Iron Heritage Centre.

Refreshments

Bradley Gardens, Sled Lane, Wylam NE41 8JH Tel. 01661 852176 Open 09:00 - 17:00.
Daniel Farm Farmshop And Tea Rooms, Wylam NE41 8JH Tel. 01661 853849
Open 09:30 - 16:30.
Cafe at Thornley Woodlands Centre is open from 10am – 2pm Mon – Fri, 1pm – 4pm
Sat and Sun. Tel. 01207 545212.
Cafe Shrub, Land of Oak and Iron Heritage Centre, Spa Well Rd, Winlaton Mill,
Blaydon-on-Tyne NE21 6RU. Tel 01207 524898.

Bradley Hall and Gardens

In the 19th century John Dobson the northern architect famed for his neoclassical and gothic architecture was commissioned to design the Bradley Hall estate for a wealthy coal mining family called the Simpsons. 1845 saw the completion of the Hall along with a 4 acre walled kitchen garden and in 1846 a local Darlington firm called Richardson's (who later who became Amdega) were asked to build a large glasshouse in the kitchen garden, allowing the family to grow more exotic fruits of the time such as pineapples, figs, lemons, grapes and oranges.

The kitchen garden had a strong team of 12 gardeners producing fruit and vegetables all year round for the family estate. As the fortunes of the times changed and the Second World War hit Britain the garden was handed over to the war effort and the local land girls worked the garden and the current car park area to produce vegetables and fruit. After the war in the 1950's the garden was sold off along with other land and property around the Estate. The garden then went on to have a variety of uses from a market garden and herb garden to later being used to graze animals on and by the 1980's the glasshouse was in a very poor state of repair and the garden had become nothing more than a field. However in 1997 the Potters bought Bradley Gardens and decided to turn it into a garden nursery, they designed a new layout for the gardens whilst preserving the few plants left around its walls. They went on to renovate the old glasshouse and turn it into a coffee shop and over a ten year period laid the bones of this once hidden gem. In 2013 the gardens were bought by local business owners Mr Crichton-Jones and Mr Robinson making it a tranquil retreat for good quality food and upmarket shopping whilst retaining the feeling of a secret garden (Bradley Gardens website).

Walk 4: Wylam to Blackhall Mill (Tyne to Derwent)

Distance	8 miles
Time	3 hours
Difficulty	Moderate
Parking	Wylam cark park or Wylam station car park
Public Transport	Trains to Wylam station, 686, X84.

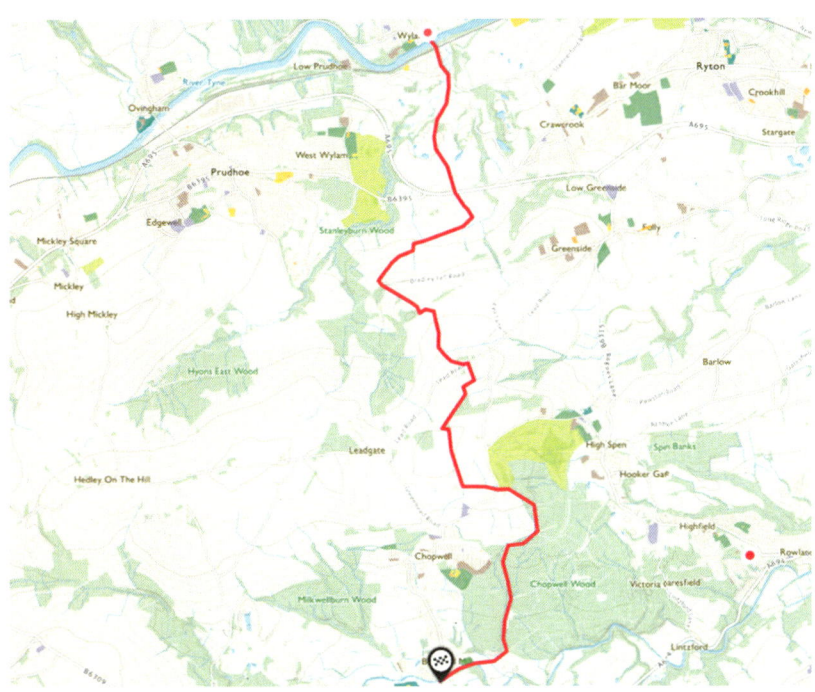

Start at the main Wylam car park on the north side of the bridge or next to Wylam station. Walk south along the road past the Boathouse pub with it on your right and follow the road for about 300 yards. Cross the road to a public footpath sign and a stile. Cross it into a field and follow the fence line, over a wooden bridge to another stile and then to the left of a deer fence then to an enclosed path through Daniel Farm. Follow this path to a double stile into a field and continue to follow the fence line through a copse to another field then to a kissing gate into a wood.

Continue through the wood to another kissing gate. Bear left uphill to a three way fingerpost. At this point follow the middle sign on the post across two fields towards a main road. Once you reach the main road, cross it to an access road and follow this road for about a mile ignoring any public footpath signs left or eight.

When you come to a steep hill walk up it for about 50 yards and there is a junction with a Restricted byway sign. Go straight ahead through the hedge to a stile and cross it following the fenceline on the left, past a house on the left. You come to another stile to an overgrown enclosed path. Follow this for about 300 yards to another stile entering a field.

Carry on uphill to another stile to the left of a small woodland. On reaching another stile turn left down a farm track and then right at a pubic footpath sign alongside a field to a farm track. Here bear left along the track uphill and just before the large pylon turn left across the field and then along the side of a copse to a stile to your right. Cross the road to a stile and a public footpath sign.

Follow the line of the hedge with it on your right to a stile. Cross another field with the hedge on your right to another stile. Turn right alongside the edge of a field and then left before the hedge to the edge of a woodland. Go across the stile into the woodland and follow the straight path, cross a stile and after 150 yards bear left to exit the woodland. Take a left onto a track then right along the edge of a field to another stile. Cross another filed to another stile. Cross it and continue along a farm track through Broomfield Farm yard and about 50 yards passed the farm buildings turn left along the farm access road. When you come to a sharp right in the access road carry straight on to a stile into a field and follow the fence line on your left to another stile.

Cross it to a road. Cross the road to a track with a green barrier across it which leads you into Chopwell woods some 200 yards ahead. On entering the trees on both sides of the path after 30 yards take the first right to a well worn path following the line of the edge of the wood for just under half a mile till you come to a wide flat path.

Turn right for about 300 yards then left down wide track for another 400 yards. When you get to a junction after a barrier take the second right track down hill (with No Admittance to unauthorised vehicles sign) which eventually turns into a narrow rough track to the right of a house. Follow this rough track for about 300 yards and take a path signposted Bridlepath Blackhall Mill to your right downhill to a bridge. Climb up the path on the other side and at the top of the steep climb turn immediately left.

Follow this path till you come to a horse and bike entrance on your left, go down the steep hill till you come to another horse and bike entrance, turn right along the track/ road to a main road. Cross it and along to the Riverside Patisserie and bakery.

Refreshments

Riverview Patisserie and Bakery, 14 Riverview, Blackhall Mill NE17 7TL
Tel 01207 563668

Wylam

The earliest reference to Wylam is in a record of 1158 that records that the settlement belonged to the priory at Tynemouth. It is thought that Guy de Balliol, Lord of Bywell, gave Wylam to the priory in 1085. The Blackett family have had a long association with the village. In 1659 Christopher Blackett acquired the Lordship of the Manor of Wylam on the death of his wife's father, Thomas Fenwick. Following Christopher's death, his second son, John Blackett, took over the estate and purchased additional land in the area, including two farms at Wylam bought in 1685. These farms formed a modest estate and residence for the Blackett family until the third quarter of the 20th century. The Lordship also included mineral rights within the township. This allowed the family to develop the colliery and further increase their prosperity.

It is thought that the Wylam waggonway was opened in 1748 and was therefore one of the earliest waggonways in the North of England. The waggonway linked the colliery to the staithes at Lemington from where the coal was taken down the River Tyne on flat bottomed boats called keels to be loaded on the large coal ships further down the river.

George Stephenson was born at a small cottage at Wylam in June 1781. Timothy Hackworth's father was foreman blacksmith at the colliery and his son was born in the village in December 1786. Hackworth together with William Hedley and Jonathan Forster were involved in the development of the locomotive engine at the colliery. Perhaps the most famous of the engines to be developed was the Puffing Billy, which is now housed at The Science Museum in London, followed closely by Wylam Dilly which is on display at the National Museum of Scotland in Edinburgh.

The late 18th century was a period of prosperity for the village – the colliery was thriving and an ironworks, a leadshot manufactury and a brewery were all established in the village. In 1864 the ironworks closed. Four years later the colliery was closed. The brewery ceased to operate sometime in the 1870s.

Chopwell Wood - See page 43

Walk 5: Path Head Water Mill and Blaydon Burn

Distance	4.9 miles
Time	2 hours
Difficulty	Easy
Parking	Cochrane Street, Summerhill or Blaydon Shopping Centre
Public Transport	10, 10A, 10B, 10X.

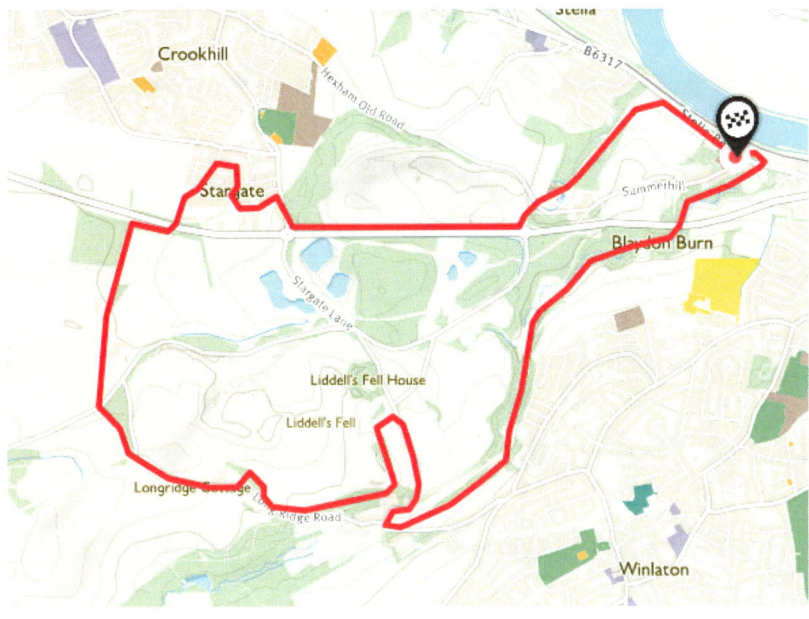

Start at Pumphreys Coffee,Summerhill. Walk west along the road away from Blaydon Centre for about 300 yards and about 30 yards after a row of houses, Caroline Terrace, bear left onto a track and head uphill through the trees on the wide track with the stream on your right and when you come to three paths ahead take the middle one and continue for about half a mile.

On exiting the wood at Path Head Water Mill go to the right of the buildings and the water wheel. This takes you to a gate, then immediately a road. Cross the road to some steep steps. Go up the steps and at the top is the entrance to a former landfill site. Cross the road to a grassy path before the roundabout.

Take this path parallel to the road for about half a mile. As you walk along this path your will look to your right and the former landfill site and its new function to produce electricity from the methane produced by the refuse underground.

At the end of this path turn right and cross the road at the obvious point and at the end of the houses turn left into Stargate Industrial Estate, cross the road to the path and in about 100 yards there is a Public Footpath sign to Cushy Cow Lane on your right just before some metal fences. Walk through the trees to a path to some houses, bear right then left along the street, left and left again and at the end of the road cross the grass to the rear of a factory unit and turn right along the path parallel to the metal fence.

Follow this path to the main road. Cross the main road (this is a busy road so be careful!). Go through the gate ahead of you and turn right following the track until you come to a public footpath sign pointing left uphill to a stile. Cross the stile onto a track and head straight along the farm track past two farmhouses.

When you come to a road, cross it to a stile and into a field. With the copse of trees on your left head straight uphill to another stile.

Cross it to a road, turn left to a roundabout and bear right up hill on the road passing the 30 mph signs. In about 300 yards immediately before Sandy Bank Lodge is a gate with a pubic footpath sign on the post. Go through the gate through a parking space to a gate with another public footpath on the post and into an enclosed grassy path. This follows the edge of the former landfill site and ends up on Liddells Fell road.

When you get to this road turn right and follow the road until you get to the bottom of the valley and turn immediately left as you approach a very tight corner signposted Keelman's Way via Blaydon.

This takes you to a track which follows Blaydon Burn down to the Tyne. At the bottom of the path go under the bridge and turn immediately right alongside the bridge to the Black Bull. Carry straight on to Blaydon Shopping Centre or turn right to Pumphrey's Coffee.

Refreshments
Pumphreys Coffee shop, Bridge Street, Blaydon NE21 4JH Tel. 0191 414 4510

Summerhill and Stella meadows
Summerhill and Stella Pastures is a designated Site of Nature Conservation Importance.

Path Head Water Mill
Started in 1730 by the Townley family, the Path Head Mill worked as a corn mill until 1828. During its working life it changed owners to the Cowen family.
Around 1974 the farm buildings became derelict, of which the later 1930's farmhouse is the only survivor. The area was then surrounded by extensive gravel extraction and only poultry survived.

In 1994 the mill pond was choked with fallen willow trees and these were removed to clear access to the building and the pond. The old corn stack terraces had their dry stone walls repaired and a pole barn was erected to cover engineering artefacts.

The water wheel was recovered from Guyzance Mill in 1994 and was stored and refurbished in the stables at City Farm before it was installed in the restored wheel pit at Path Head in 1997, ready for the mill opening in March 1998. The stonework for the headrace and overflow channel was rebuilt using recovered stone from a demolished railway bridge in Byker. Since then the grounds and buildings have been developed to what you see today (Path Head water mill website)

Stargate Ponds and Bewes Hills

Stargate Ponds and Bewes Hills is an area reclaimed from former quarrying and opencast activities. It is an important area for many species of plants, birds and insects.

Blaydon Burn

Once the heart of the industrial revolution in Gateshead, Blaydon Burn is a wonderful example of what happens when industry moves away and nature returns. Over one mile long and covering over 50 hectares of woodland, grassland and wetland, Blaydon Burn is a treasure trove of industrial archaeology and wildlife waiting to be discovered. Bronze Age people lived at nearby Summer Hill and people have been living and working in Blaydon Burn since the Middle Ages.

Initially, the key to the industrial development at Blaydon Burn was water power and by the 18th century at least eight corn mills were operating along its length.

From the 19th century industrial development expanded rapidly to include a number of industries related to the processing of coal. The supply of cheap local fuel and good transport links led to the development of coke works, steelworks, iron foundries and brickworks making Blaydon Burn one of the most industrialised parts of the region. However, from the 1950s advances in technology, declining local raw materials and overseas competition saw the decline and closure of the industries in Blaydon Burn. In the 70s and 80s the Ottovale Works were reclaimed, Cowen's Lower Yard was cleared, the Blaydon Burn Waggonway was taken up and the Burn was largely left to return to nature.

Today, the remnants of the area's industrial history can still be seen in the 108 different stone and brick-built features which are scattered throughout the nature reserve and in the historical records which make Blaydon Burn one of the most important sites for the study of industrial archaeology in the north east.

Pockets of oak and birch woodland survived all the years of industrial activity and later acted as seed banks for reclaiming the abandoned industrial areas.

Five small leaved lime trees also survived the industrial revolution and are now over 300 years old. This tree reaches its northern limit in Gateshead and there are only about 300 small leaved lime trees in north east England.

A wide range of birds also live in the woodland including, green woodpecker, tawny owl, woodcock, willow warbler and sparrowhawk.

The Burn itself flows underground through much of the site, emerging for only short stretches. Despite Blaydon Burn's industrial past, the water itself is very clean, containing a variety of invertebrates such as mayfly and freshwater shrimps (Gateshead Council).

Walk 6: Woodhouse Lane and Derwenthaugh Park

Distance	5.2 miles
Time	2 hours
Difficulty	Moderate
Parking	Swalwell Centre car park
Public Transport	6, 6A, M6, M7, M8, 69B, 841

Begin at Pedalling Squares cafe on Whickham bank. Cross the road from the cafe and head up the road signed 'Clockburn 1¾ miles'. Bear left at the fork, this is Woodhouse lane. Within about 150 yards the road ends and merges with a track. At the top of the hill is path behind some houses. Bear right along this path and head along this track for about 1¼ miles.

As the path rises, in about 100yards take a right turn through a stile next to a gate and bear diagonally right across the field to another stile then through an enclosed path between two fences of a stable area. Turn right down the hill on a wide track (ignoring the C2C sign to the Derwent Walk) and keep left along the wide track to a farm. As you approach the farm keep the farm buildings to your left and turn towards agate on your right and follow the line of the fence with it on your right.

Cross the stile just after the last building and head diagonally left for another stile and onto a path where you turn left up some steps heading towards Hollinside Manor. On the other side of the manor there are some steep steps down to some duckboards. This path takes you to the Derwent Walk. On reaching the walk turn left, and in about 50 yards turn right. Take the left tarmaced path and head downhill eventually following the riverbank to a bridge.

Cross the bridge and straight on are the remains of Crowley's works. You could take this path on the left or you could turn right around the lake coming to the same point as if you had taken the left turn. On reaching that point in about 100 yards the Butterfly bridge is on your right. Carry on down this path to pass the Land of Oak and Iron visitor centre.
Carry on down this path past Swalwell Football Club, Blaydon Tennis Club and Swalwell Cricket Club. Also on your right you pass a weir with the fish pass and site of the Derwenthaugh Coke works.

As you pass under a road bridge in about 50 yards turn right across a stone bridge and follow this road to the main road to Swalwell cross the road and follow it to the bottom of Whickham bank and up to Pedalling Squares or the car park.

Refreshments
Cafe Shrub, Land of Oak and Iron Heritage Centre, Spa Well Rd, Winlaton Mill, Blaydon-on-Tyne NE21 6RU. Tel 01207 524898.
Pedalling Squares Coffee Bar, Quality Row, Swalwell NE16 3AQ. Tel. 0191 5972245.

Woodhouse Lane and Hollinside Manor

Woodhouses Lane is an ancient waggonway between Swalwell and the Gibside estate. Hollinside Manor is a 13th century manor house and was the home of the Harding family for two centuries during which time the manor became known as the 'Giant's Castle' since the men folk were very tall. The estate passed on to George Bowes of Gibside in 1730 for the sum of £10,000. Today the Manor is an Ancient Monument. The earliest mention of the place occurs in 1317. It belonged to a family of the name of Hollinside and on March 13th, 1318, Thomas Hollinside conveyed his manor of Hollinside, near Axwell, to William Bointon, or de Boyneton, of Newcastle, and Isolda, his wife, with all his lands, and free service of his tenants, a watermill called Clokinthenns, on the New Dene Burn, and his fishery in the Derwent.

The name Clokinthenns is a slightly corrupted form as Clockburn. The mill mentioned as existing in 1318; is evidently a predecessor of the present Clockburn Mill which stands a little to the west of the Manor House.

Hollinside next passed into the hands of the Burdon or Burton fancily, and then by marriage to the Redheughs, a wealthy northern family whose name is still preserved in the Redheugh Bridge across the Tyne at Gateshead. Then it passed to the Massams or Mashams, who were also possessors of part of Gibside, and next to the Harding family. About 1430, Roger Harding, a burgess of Newcastle, and a descendant of Sampson Harding, who was Mayor of Newcastle from 1396 to 1399, and who was also M.P., acquired the Hollinside Manor by marriage, and it remained in his family until 1730, when owing to their shattered fortune; they had been obliged to mortgage their estates to the Bowes family of Gibside, and it passed to that family by foreclosure and subsequent conveyance. It still forms a portion of the Gibside estate. (GenUKI)

Crowleys Works

In 1690 Ambrose Crowley relocated to Winlaton, possibly because the local coal was particularly suitable to iron working and the availability of charcoal. It is not proven but it seems probable he was given backing by Sir William Bowes of Gibside Hall. In the late 1690s local ads for labour sought 'good workmen who can make the following goods for which they will receive constant employment and wages paid punctually every week - augers, bed-screws, box and sad irons, chains, edge tools, files, hammers, hinges, hoes for the plantation, locks (specially ho-locks), nails, patten-rings and all other sorts of smith work'. (Bourn)

The ironworks (or 'The Factory' as it was known) was extended to Winlaton Mill (formerly Huntlayshaugh before Crowley arrived and set up the iron works where there had been a flour and fulling mill, on which he took a 99 year lease). Crowley recruited more skilled men in London and brought them north. In 1707, at Swalwell, a rival enterprise was bought out, bringing 'The Factory' to its full expansion. Smaller items were made at Winlaton, which was also the headquarters till the mid eighteenth century. Larger forgings (such as anchors and whaling harpoons) were made at Swalwell and Winlaton Mill. By 1712 Crowley was prepared to make any type of ironware.

At its peak 1500 men were employed. Smithy shops (built in communal groups and laid out in squares) were erected in every part of the village - nail makers, chain makers, hinge makers and so on. The goods made were sent to his Blaydon warehouse, loaded onto keels and taken to his 'New Quay' at Newcastle, then shipped, much of it to his large warehouse facility at Greenwich. The Admiralty was his major customer and indeed from 1690 to 1815/16 a substantial proportion of Admiralty procured ironmongery was supplied by the Crowley business.

Initially working hours were long - between 5am and 8pm (with a 9pm curfew) but Crowley looked after his workers as much as he could.

He took interest in the religious welfare of his workers, had a chapel built by 1706 with money raised by subscription. The surplus was applied to the maintenance of a public school. He initiated social care for his workers' families from cradle to grave. Schooling was important such that the area near the school became known locally as 'knowledge hill'. Medical care was provided too. Workers agreed to subscriptions from wages and together with donations from Crowley this enabled weekly pensions to the retired, including widows and regular payments also to those who were injured or in ill health. Those getting help were called 'Crowley's Poor' and wore a badge. The ethos was - work hard and you will be looked after!

Crowley's Court

This was set up to meet every ten weeks, to deal with disputes among the workers. A code of laws and rules was developed and covered matters such as debt, complaints, misdemeanours. The tribunal decisions were binding - there was no appeal. Any payments would probably be by a regular deduction from pay in accord with the judgement. Non compliance meant expulsion. This strict regime ensured a relatively content workforce who knew 'the rules' and what they could and could not do.

The business thrived and Crowley became a wealthy man in the process, eventually being knighted, in 1706. He had never made Tyneside his home but was a frequent visitor. He would send copious and detailed instructions to his managers. He was a Freeman of the Drapers Company and its Master in 1707. A career in politics followed - he served as Sheriff of London in 1707, then became an alderman of the City of London, then he was elected MP for Andover but sadly he died suddenly in 1713, before he could take up his seat in Parliament. He is buried at the Parish Church, Mitcham in Surrey. The firm which Crowley founded was continued by his son John (who also inherited the grandfather's business at Stourbridge) and then by his grandsons and lasted well into the reign of Queen Victoria, prospering from all the wars in the century following his death (Roly Vietch http://www.rolyveitch.20m.com/CrowleyCrew.html)

Derwenthaugh Coke Works

This was a coking plant on the River Derwent. The works were built in 1928 on the site of the Crowley's Iron Works. The coke works was closed and demolished in the late 1980s, and replaced by Derwenthaugh Park (wikipaedia).

Walk 7: Shibdon Pond, Blaydon Burn, Lands Wood

Distance	6.7 miles
Time	2.5 hours
Difficulty	Moderate
Parking	Land of Oak and Iron Heritage Centre
Public Transport	45, 46 or 47

Begin at Land of Oak and Iron Centre from the carpark walk behind the centre and onto the Derwent Walk. Turn left down the walk towards Swalwell for about 1 ½ miles. When you pass under a road bridge after about 50 yards turn left towards the main road. When you get to it turn right to a pedestrian crossing. Cross this and head back towards the roundabout and turn right along the road which heads towards Blaydon. You pass the Blaydon Primary Care Centre and Leisure Centre and rather large house on the right.

Continue along the road side path towards the open green area which is by Shibdon pond. After a low stone wall bear right towards Shibdon pond keeping right till you come to its shore. Continue towards the boardwalk and at the end of it turn right to a gate. Go through the gate which takes you to a long boardwalk over the pond.

At the end of the boardwalk there is a gate, after it bear right to a large pylon. At the next gate follow the electricity pylons and as you get to a right turn under the A1, ignore it, and head left along a wide path to a gate and tarmaced road. Here you pass a Recycling centre at Cowen road. Follow the road keeping right and at the T junction with Morrison's garage on your left, turn right to go under a flyover and across a railway crossing. Immediately after the railway crossing, cross the road to turn left along the road past the signal box on your left to a path alongside the Tyne.

Follow this path till you get to a low railway bridge on your left. Go under this and carry on under a blue road bridge onto the Blaydon Burn path. Follow this path for about a mile to the top of Blaydon Burn Nature reserve. As you exit Blaydon Burn turn left up the roadside path and in about 40 yards turn right to a rough track towards a path to the right of an industrial enclosure.

Follow the path around this enclosure and as you turn left you come to an enclosed path up the hillside crossing over several stiles till you get to a road. Cross the road and onto a path with the houses on your left and open fields to the right (Knobbyends Lane). Follow this path till you come to a sharp left hand bend. Just before the metal fence next to the path bear right down a steep grass verge to cross the road to a public footpath sign to your left. At the bottom of the field turn left along the edge of the field to a stile then to another stile in a white fence in the bottom right hand corner.

This takes you onto an access road. Turn right down to the main road. Turn left up the roadside path for about 100 yards, and before the 30 mph sign cross the road to a path which takes you to the right of some houses and garages with fields on your right. Follow this path to the end of the houses and turn right on reaching houses in front of you. Follow this to an enclosed pathway. At the entrance to this pathway turn immediately left and diagonally across the field into a wood. Keep to the left path as you enter the wood. When you come to a four path junction take the one straight ahead.

Keeping left you when you come to a fence on your left, carry on to an enclosed path between the houses. Bear left when you get to the estate road, to a path to the left of a house. Follow this path down steps keeping left alongside the dene to the main road. Cross the road and turn right to the Land of Oak and Iron Heritage Centre.

Refreshments

Cafe Shrub, Land of Oak and Iron Heritage Centre, Spa Well Rd, Winlaton Mill, Blaydon-on-Tyne NE21 6RU. Tel 01207 524898.
Pumphreys Coffee Shop, Bridge Street, Blaydon NE21 4JH Tel. 0191 414 4510.

Derwenthaugh Cokeworks

Derwenthaugh Coke Works was a coking plant on the River Derwent. The works were built in 1928 on the site of the Crowley's Iron Works. The coke works was closed and demolished in the late 1980s, and replaced by Derwenthaugh Park (wikipaedia).

Shibdon Pond

In the nineteenth century this site had been a series of wetland pastures, but this changed when twentieth century mining and railway activities altered the water level and formed the pond. Between 1837 and 1951 Blaydon Main Colliery dominated the site. The capped shaft can still be seen behind Blaydon Swimming Pool. This area used to be a refuse dump, but careful planting and management of native British trees have ensured a rich new habitat for the future. Many birds are attracted to the pond including Swans, Canada Geese, Moorhens, Coot etc. There are also Exmoor ponies on the shores who keep the scrubland in good condition. The grassland provides habitat for voles and shrews which attract hunting kestrels.

Blaydon Burn – See page 30

Winlaton Forge

Is the last surviving link in the village with Crowley's Iron Works. Ambrose Crowley's works at Winlaton Mill dominated the iron manufacturing trade in the North East throughout the 18th Century, and at Swalwell were probably, at the time, Europe's biggest industrial location. This small forge behind the library in Winlaton has been preserved. The forge is a Grade II listed building (Co-curate website).

Walk 8: Rowlands Gill, Spen Burn, Hookergate, Victoria Garesfield, Whinfield Coke Ovens

Distance	5 miles
Time	1.45 hours
Difficulty	Easy
Parking	Viaduct car park off Burnopfield Road
Public Transport	45, 46 or 47

Start at the car park next to the Viaduct off Stirling Lane, Rowlands Gill. Walk up towards the viaduct but turn immediately left before reaching it (do not cross the viaduct). Follow this path to the road (Stirling Lane), cross it and follow the path along Burnopfield road to the junction with the main road through Rowlands Gill.
Cross the road immediately before the bus stop and cross the Green heading to a signpost at the centre left of the edge of the Green. Follow Blaydon 120 sign and pass through the horse gate and kissing gate.

Follow the path for about 300 yards to a path on the right hand side down the bank to a bridge. Cross the bridge and follow the path up the other side of the valley or take the steps to the left. Walk along this wide path for about 1 and half miles.

On reaching the road bear left up the hill passing the former Hookergate school site on your left. Carry on till you come to some houses on your right, this is Robson Terrace. Turn right into the cul de sac to a stile. Cross it and follow the line of the fence on your left and bear left up a hill till you come to another stile leading to an enclosed path at the rear of a terrace of houses (Wood Terrace)

This will take you to a road (Hookergate Lane). Cross the road and head up the road passed a no through road sign and keep to the right hand path with a small estate of house to your right (Beechwood). Follow the path and at the top of the hill there is a path to the right of the road which goes left, follow this till you come to a cottage. Take the road to its left and follow this road for about 100 yards and take the path to the left which indicates a path to the car park and follow it for about 400 yards. At the end of this path is a wooden arch, immediately after it turn left and in about another 30 yards turn left again and follow this path for another 500 yards.

When you come to a T junction take the left turn doing a U turn and snaking around to a gate. Go through the gate and head left up the road keeping the houses on your right. At the T junction turn right following a tarmaced and rough track then a tarmaced road till you come to a dead end.

Turn sharp left at the end of the road and follow the path with the fence on your right. (do not go through the kissing gate) Follow this path to the road (Lintzford Lane). On reaching the road turn right then in about 10 yards turn left down some steps and follow this path for about 500 yards to enter the Whinfield industrial estate hammer head. Immediately on your right is the entrance to the Whinfield coke ovens.

Follow the estate road for about 100 yards and bear left then right and follow this road for about 500 yards to the main road.

Cross the road and turn right (Smailes lane). Carry on along the path for another 100 yards and carry on straight ahead following the path for another 300 yards. Turn left when you get to where the road goes sharply downhill hill. Cross the green and head for the white flat roofed building (Rowlands Gill Library – stop for a coffee!).

When you get to the library, turn right heading to the shops on the main road. Cross the road at the pedestrian crossing and take the right hand road to the side of Tesco's and follow this road back to the car park.

Refreshments
Cafe in the old CO-OP buildings, Hookergate.
Rowlands Gill Library, Norman road, Rowlands Gill.
The Kitchen, Station Road, Rowlands Gill.

Chopwell Woods
Chopwell Wood is a 360-hectare mixed woodland. It has miles of paths for walking, cycling and riding into the heart of this wonderful woodland.

Chopwell Woodland Park was once part of an extensive forest area which covered the countryside from just south of the River Tyne to Allenheads. This so called Wildwood formed about 6000 years ago and consisted of mixed deciduous trees, mainly oak and hazel.

By the 12th century the wood was part of the Manor of Ceoppa's weille (named by the Saxons) which belonged to the Church. After the dissolution of the monasteries the Crown granted or leased the Manor. Timber from Chopwell was used throughout the 16th and 17th centuries to repair castles and bridges in Northumberland and Durham. In 1635 over 1000 trees were marked for construction of a new war ship for King Charles I – "Sovereign of the Seas", later renamed as "The Royal Sovereign".

At the beginning of the 19th century much of the wood was replanted with Oak, but in 1825 an invasion of mice caused a lot of damage by gnawing down many young oaks! Then on January 7th 1839, 20,000 trees were uprooted on "Windy Monday". During the second half of the 19th century much of the wood was planted with Larch and some Scots Pine. The wood was drift under-mined in the 19th and early 20th centuries for coal deposits, and a mineral rail-line ran through the wood.

In 1907, Armstrong College, which later became Newcastle University, took on the management of the wood as a demonstration area and training ground for foresters. In 1919 the Forestry Commission took over management of the wood, with the College still dealing as agents for the current stock. They began a full scale replanting programme. Much of the replanting was coniferous, but with some small groups of deciduous trees.

During the Second World War, in October 1941, a German Bomber dropped three high explosive bombs on the Wood, creating three deep craters. These filled with water and have become an excellent wildlife habitat over the years, mainly due to the depth of the original craters!

With the designation of Woodland Park status in 1993, a much greater emphasis has been placed upon conservation and recreation. The commercial forestry is carried out with a more sympathetic manner to these aims. In 2005 the Wood was designated under the PAWS (Plantation on an Ancient Woodland Site) scheme, which prohibits further planting of any trees not native to the area. The Forest Design Plan for Chopwell Wood instructs natural regeneration of species after any felling, or planting of native species only. Keep an eye for deer which are regularly seen in these woods (Friends of Chopwell Wood).

Victoria Garesfield

The first reports of mining in the Chopwell area date back before the 14th century. A pit was also worked here from 1605 – 1645. These pits would probably have been bell pits, the miners accessing seams near the surface. The first deep pit was the Maria pit near Greymore Hill, started in 1756, and by 1767 there was Whitefield Colliery near Chopwell, producing 31,800 tons per year.

1765 was the year that saw the beginning of the 'Garesfield' pits with the opening of a pit near Ash Tree farm, Low Spen, followed by, in 1801, the opening of one on land effectively belonging to a certain Mr Gair and known as 'Gair's Field' at High Thornley by the Marquis of Bute.

The pit at 'Gair's Field' produced excellent coking coal and the name evolved into Garesfield and by 1819 there were four pits working, known as Garesfield numbers 1, 2, 3 and 4. In 1837, the pit at Garesfield farm closed and a new drift was started at High Spen called Garesfield Bute Pit (ownership passing to the Consett Iron Company in 1890). Other collieries were later opened nearby and used the Garesfield name as a mark of quality of their own coal and name.

Victoria Garesfield Colliery was developed in 1870 just south of Beda Hills and adjacent to Lintzford Lane, by a local farmer and landowner named Thomas Ramsay. In April 1876 Messrs Priestman and Peile took a controlling interest and the colliery came under the ownership of the Victoria Garesfield Colliery Company.

In 1899 Victoria Garesfield was one of four collieries along with Lilley Drift, Blaydon Burn and Waldrige that were amalgamated under 'Owners of Priestman Collieries' with Messrs Priestman and Peil running the operation.

The Priestman Coal Company, as it became, would seem to have been a charitable employer, investing in its workers' welfare. In 1883 at Victoria Garesfield it opened a reading room and a mixed school for some 200 pupils. Known as 'the British School Victoria Garesfield', it operated under a system which allowed for the tuition of the masses of children by older partially educated children with a minimum of staff. By 1851, the British School in Victoria Garesfield was one of 1,500 such schools in the country.

The building of the school was followed by that of the chapel in 1885/1886, the construction of which the colliery owners supported through the donation of bricks

from their brickworks. A school-room was later added to the chapel in 1904. Priestman Collieries Ltd. also provided rent-free accommodation and allotments for their workers at Victoria Garesfield, along with free electricity and free coal for heating.

Brickworks

Along with coal, fire-clay was also extracted at Victoria Garesfield (most coal seams having an underlying layer of clay). From 1875 to 1928 a firebrick works operated in the colliery yard at Victoria Garesfield, producing a ready source of building materials and employing some twenty or so workers.

The hand-molded bricks produced here were marked V.G.C. and were used in the construction of various buildings and houses erected at the colliery. The bricks were light-buff/yellow in colour, a type then common across the Durham coal field.

When the colliery closed in 1962, the people of the village dispersed to the surrounding villages where council house were available. A pattern of destruction followed which had occurred with the closure of the Spen pit two years previously but the destruction was more complete, all of the ducketts and many of the other houses were demolished and the colliery buildings levelled, the chapel survived an extra year to be demolished in 1963. The National Coal Board returned the land to the Forestry Commission and then nature took over. Only a few of the houses remain - two terraces and the school houses split by an expanse of woodland.

The Victoria Garesfield Colliery Tubway

Although some coal was used locally, most of it had to be transported to the River Tyne. This was done using wagonways or tubways, which carried coal wagons or smaller coal tubs. These were the first railways and were in use from about 1650 in North East England. The wagonways were first made of wood and the wagons and tubs were drawn by horses or could go down hill under their own weight controlled by a brake worked by the driver, called the waggoner.

As technology developed wooden rails were replaced with iron rails and mechanical haulage systems replaced horses. A tubway with iron rails was used in the tunnels of the drift mine at Victoria Garesfield. Starting in 1860, eventually three main tunnels were dug together with two remote access drifts. One of these tunnels, called the "The Coronation Drift" or "West Way", went right under Chopwell Wood from Victoria Garesfield coming to the surface in a cutting close to Chopwell. Men returning to the area after the First World War found work in this drift mine tunnel, and it became known locally as "The Barracks".

From the screens as Victoria Garesfield colliery where the coal arrived in tubs, it was loaded into coal wagons on the railway, the colliery being linked by a 1.5 mile branch railway line to the North Eastern Railway just north of Rowlands Gill station.

Whinfield Cokeworks

As much of the coal in the Chopwell and High Spen area was high quality coking coal, ideal for the malleable iron founding industries of County Durham, in 1861/2 the Marquis of Bute had 193 bee-hive coke ovens built at Whinfield, half a mile from Victoria Garesfield on the track which took their coal to the Tyne. Whilst these ovens had initially been supplied from Chopwell, with the opening of Victoria Garesfield colliery in 1870, it in turn became the main supplier, most of the coking coal extracted from its Victoria and Brockwell seams. A wagon way to transport the coal from Victoria Garesfield to Whinfield was built the same year the colliery opened and remained in operation until 1962.

At the height of operations, the Whinfield works produced some 68 000 tonnes of coke per year (https://victoriagaresfield.weebly.com/history.html).

Walk 9: Lintz Green and Pont Burn woods

Distance	6 miles
Time	2.5 hours
Difficulty	Moderate
Parking	Layby on A694 Lintzford Road just past the Lintzford houses on the left before the bridge over the River Derwent.
Public Transport	45 or 46

Walk back towards the houses at Lintzford and turn right across the bridge towards the houses and bear right up the track between the houses passing a bungalow on the right about 100 yards on.

This was the path between the Lintzford Mill and Lintz Green station. This wide path narrows to a dirt path and eventually widens again further up the hill.

At the top of the hill continue straight on across the bridge above the Derwent walk with the former station house on the left. You are now passing over the former Lintz Green Station. Carry on till you get to the houses of Lintz Green next to a road. Turn left and cross the road and take the road to Lintz Hall Farm on your right.

Follow this road/ track uphill ignoring any side public footpath signs for about ¾ mile until you get to a farm where the track levels out where five tracks meet. Turn right between the farm outbuildings onto a farm track. Follow this track for about 1.5 miles along the contour, heading towards Pontop Pike mast and later Pontop Hall. There are lovely views over Chopwell woods and the middle part of the valley.

Along this stretch you go through several gates and stiles. Head for a small woodland going through it on the obvious path and bridge over a stream. Cross the stile out of the wood and across the track to another stile following the public footpath sign. Cross this field to a stile next to a gate.

Cross the stile heading towards the large house, Pontop Hall, in the distance. Head for another stile and then a bridge and after the bridge turn right down a track through woodland. When you reach a pond on your right bear left along the wide track and follow this for about a mile crossing over a bridge over the Pont Burn with an information panel about the Mystery of the Pont Burn Stones.

As you emerge from the woodland there is a gate onto an enclosed farm track leading to a tarmaced road across a bridge over a small gorge. Follow this estate road to the main road and cross straight over the road to a path under the Viaduct following the track through some houses and onto the A694 road where you turn right down the hill to the layby and welcome refreshment at the Lintzford Garden Centre Cafe.

Refreshments

Lintzford Garden Centre, Lintzford Bridge Garden Centre Lintzford Road, Rowlands Gill NE39 1DG, Tel. 01207 549777, Open 09:00 - 17:00

Lintzford Mill

In 1881, Messrs. E H and Arthur Richardson (who were involved in importing resin for the manufacture of printing ink) founded a company, E H and A Richardson, to manufacture printing ink. On 12 July 1888, this was registered and renamed as Richardson and Harrison Ltd, with directors E H, Arthur and C J Richardson and D W Harrison. Their factory was Team Valley Works, Gateshead. On 31 May 1893, the company was again renamed the Richardson Printing Ink Company Limited. They remained at the Team Valley works until 1926, when they took over a paper mill at Lintzford, Rowlands Gill, where they remained until the 1980s when they relocated to Washington and the south of England. They were able to manufacture inks of unlimited colours to exact specifications. They were also involved with the Hooghly Ink Company Limited in Calcutta.

The site of water corn mill dating back to the 14th century but making paper possibly from 1695, certainly by 1703. It was a paper mill of some importance for hand made paper by 1800. Continued making paper until 1922-4 when an ink works were established on the site. Originally water, but later steam powered. Richardson's Printing Inks was converted to residential use in 1987.

Lintzford Bridge leads into a courtyard with setted carriageway. The former ink works are now known as Turbine House, which has been partially demolished to make way for a central green. On the northern side of the courtyard is Lintzford House, the mill owner's residence, now converted into two houses. On the riverside behind the former ink works is a former mill, now a house. Opposite this is a terrace of workmen's cottages. The mill race, dating to 1840, survives on the southern side of the courtyard, screened by a high stone wall. The race has sandstone steps and a sluice. Adjacent to the bridge are two houses, Bridge House (18th century) and Mill House (a 1989 copy).

The bridge is a remarkable coursed squared sandstone-built road bridge with single, very wide flat segmental arch whose voussoirs noticeably increase in size from crown to springings. Each spandrel pierced four times with diminishing circular holes in the style of Edward's 1756 bridge at Pontypridd (http://twsitelines.info)

Lintz Green Station

Work on the Derwent Valley Railway started in 1865 and the line was opened on 2nd December 1867. Four viaducts were constructed and a deep, 800 metres long cutting was dug near Rowlands Gill. The Nine Arches Viaduct was one of the major engineering feats of the railway; it is five hundred feet long and was built because the Earl of Strathmore would not allow the railway to pass through the Gibside Estate. Stations were built at Blackhill, Shotley Bridge, Ebchester, Lintz Green, Rowlands Gill and Swalwell with High Westwood added in 1909. The line was single track between Blackhill and Lintz Green and double track between Lintz Green and the junction at Derwenthaugh. At its peak in 1914 the railway was carrying over half a million passengers a year with a regular goods traffic of timber, bricks and coal to Newcastle and iron ore to Consett.

The line also has a gruesome claim to fame in 1911 Lintz Green station was the scene of the inexplicable murder of the stationmaster by an unknown gunman, the crime never solved.

Lintz Green closed in December 1953. The line finally closed completely on 11th November 1963.The track was lifted in 1964 and for many years little was done to the line until Durham County Council developed it as a country park. The viaducts and bridges were repaired and the trackbed has now become an excellent cycle route and country path.

Lintz Hall Farm

The Tulip family first became involved in farming during the second world war when George Tulip was co-opted into the "Dig for Britain" campaign.

In 1963 the family moved to Lintz Hall Farm and the original site of 120 acres, now extends to 600.Lintz Hall now employs over 50 people, and is home to many thousands of birds,sheep and horses.

The main focus of the business is, as always, poultry and egg production. Lintz Hall's brand eggs are now delivered all over the North East of England by their fleet of delivery vehicles. The customer base is diverse, and ranges from supermarket chains to corner shops, hospitals, local authorities, hotels and restaurants.

Pont Burn Stones and Hamsterley Hall

These stones are boundary stones erected in the early 19th century to mark the boundaries of the Pontop estate owned by the Swinburne family. They are carved with the letter 'P'. Later they were carved with the letters 'CIC' because the land was purchased by the Consett Iron Company. 33 stones were erected but only 16 have been discovered.

Hamsterley Hall is an 18th-century English country house and a Grade II listed building. The estate at Hamsterley was given, in 1762, by Sir John Swinburne to his younger brother Henry Swinburne. In 1769, Henry carried out substantial alterations to the house to create the present two-story, four-bayed castelled Gothic Revival-style mansion.

Swinburne died in 1803 and in 1806 the property was sold to Anthony Surtees. His son Robert Smith Surtees, a novelist, acquired the estate in 1838. He was High Sheriff of Durham in 1856. He died in 1864, leaving his estate to his daughter Eleanor, who married John Gage Prendergast Vereker, 5th Viscount Gort in 1885. Their first son John Vereker, 6th Viscount Gort VC was succeeded in 1946 by his brother Standish Vereker, 7th Viscount MC who lived at Hamsterley until his death in 1975.

Walk 10: Milkwellburn woods, Vindomara and Derwentcote steel furnace

Distance	7.8 miles
Time	3.5 hours
Difficulty	Moderate
Parking	Street parking in Blackhall Mill
Public Transport	45, 46 or 47

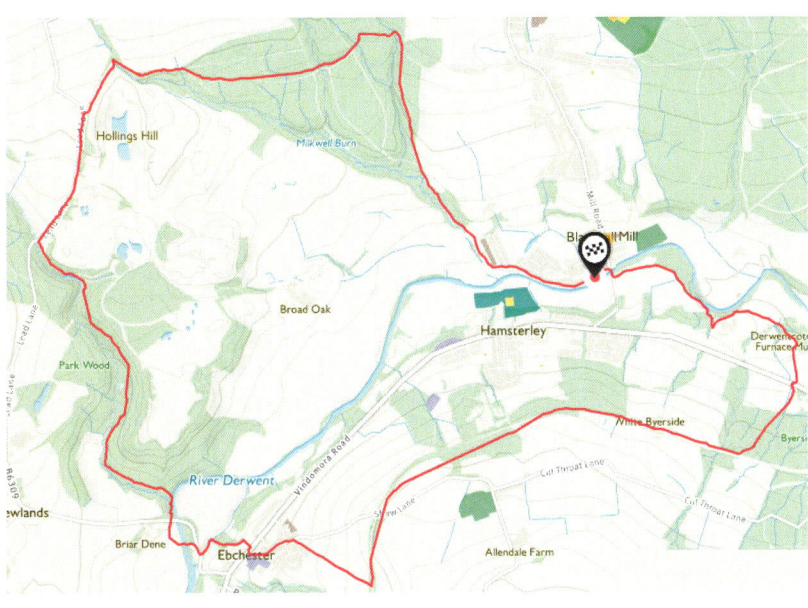

Start at the Riverview Bakery on River view, Blackhall Mill. Walk along the road,with the river on your left, to the end of the road. Pass the terraced houses on your right to a track and after about 50 yards the track bends right away from the river. It follows a stream on the left. In about 150 yards there are three tracks, take the middle one for ½ mile. This is the public bridleway signpost to Milkwellburn wood.

When you come to fork in the track turn right and carry on uphill and at the top of the hill there is a four way crossroad, turn left slightly downhill to a kink in the path across a stream and steeply uphill for about 30 yards.

Carry on straight ahead ignoring any left or right tracks for about quarter of a mile. At a 4 way junction carry on ahead to a narrower path for a further half a mile. Follow this path till you come to a fence and continue with the fence on your right. Follow the fenceline till is veers away from the fence through the wood for a short distance keeping left to an open area to the right of a quarry.

Follow the path with the quarry on your left until you come to a road. Turn left down the road to the bottom of the hill. Turn left at a public right of way sign for Ebchester 1¼ miles.

Follow the path down the valley with the stream on your right bearing right at any fork in the path. When you come to a road bridge go under it and right up hill to a gate. This takes you into an enclosed path and another gate. Turn left downhill to an old road bridge. Cross it and then turn right and cross the road to a track to the right of a house. (Detour to Postick mill - the weir). Follow this lane for about 100 yards and take the right hand turn to a public footpath and follow it up hill on steps to come to a gap between a children's playground and a garden fence. On reaching the road, cross it to Shaw Lane next to the church. Follow Shaw Lane for about 250 yards and take a right turn between houses up a wide path up to the Derwent walk.

On reaching the wide path of the Derwent Walk turn left along the walk for about a mile crossing one road and soon after, a rough track. Soon after the rough track you walk under a bridge and about 400 yards passed the bridge take a left turn to a path through a wood and on emerging from the wood turn left till you come to a road.

Cross the road and take a left turn passed a bungalow, this land takes you to the Derwentcote Steel Furnace. On passing the ironworks at the bottom of the hill if you take a right this takes you to the Derwentcote workers cottages. But take a left across a stream to a stile, a small enclosure and another stile. Cross this and follow the path across the meadow going slightly uphill to a stile to an enclosed path which eventually opens out to a wider area.

At the end of this enclosed area turn immediately right downhill towards the river and turn left alongside the river till you come to the bridge over the River Derwent. Cross the bridge turn left back to the River View Bakery.

Refreshments

Riverview Patisserie and Bakery, 14 Riverview, Blackhall Mill NE17 7TL Tel 01207 563668

Blackhall Mill

In the early eighteenth century, Blackhall Mill changed from a mainly rural estate to a steel making village.

The Bertram family operated a steel forge from the early 1700s. It was visited by Swedish engineers, Kalmeter in 1719 and Angerstein in 1754. They visited the papermill which was operated by the same millrace as the forge. Angerstein, on his visit in 1754 was studying new methods of industrial technology. There is reference to a smelt mill at Blackhall Mill in an indenture of 1773, and Mr. William Bertram of Ryton parish was owner or part owner of the sword factory at Blackhall Mill at the same period. The Blackhall Mill steel forge (later the site of the council school) used power from a dam across the Derwent near Beechgrove Terrace (www.ourgateshead.org).

Milkwellburn Woods

Formally an ancient semi-natural woodland, the diverse flora and fauna of this ancient oak wood remain in the woods' steep sided gills. Streams and springs support a rich moss and fern community. Conifer plantation has replaced broadleaf woodland on the gentler slopes, but a program of restoration by the Durham WildlifeTrust now breathes new life into these areas (Durham Wildlife Trust).

Vindomora

Vindomora (or Ebchester Roman Fort) was probably an earth and timber fort built in about AD 80 to protect Dere street. The stone fort was built in AD163 but was abandoned in AD410. Little remains of the fort as the village was built directly on top of it. Roman remains are spread amongst the gardens, cottages, roads and St.Ebba's Church. Parts of the walls are still visible near the post office (Wikipaedia).

Derwentcote Steel Furnace

This was built in the 1730s and was used for cementation, a process which converted wrought iron into steel.

It is one of the few complete examples of this type of furnace, and is the last surviving piece of evidence of cementation steelmaking in the north-east.
The conical chimney houses two sandstone chests into which iron bars were packed with alternate layers of charcoal powder.

When the fire was lit and the chests sealed, flames and heat travelled up through flues and chimneys around them, and temperatures reached 1,100°C. This heat enabled the carbon from the charcoal to diffuse into the iron.

Each cementation cycle, or 'heat', took three weeks, producing about 10 tons of steel. The firing took 6 - 10 days and the furnace was then allowed to cool for a week, before the bars could be extracted.

These bars of 'blister steel' were taken to the nearby water-powered forge, to be made into items such as cutting tools and springs. The steel had remarkable flexibility and strength, and was said to be of excellent quality.

The Derwent valley was the centre of the British steel industry in the early 18th century, as it had all the natural resources needed for the cementation process. It had plentiful supplies of charcoal, coal, clay and sandstone, and easy access to the North Sea for the import of Swedish iron.

Derwentcote furnace went out of use by 1891 and subsequently fell into disrepair. It was restored by English Heritage in 1990 (http://www.english-heritage.org.uk)

Walk 11: Consett, Hownsgill, Allensford and Shotley Bridge

Distance	7.8 miles
Time	3/4 hours
Difficulty	Easy (Difficult last mile)
Parking	St Aidans street, Blackhill, Consett
Public Transport	45 or 46

Start at the Lodge, a white building near the gates, in Blackhill and Consett Park. Head out of the park towards the church and cross the road and walk down St Aidan's Street to the grassy area at the bottom of the street. There are 2 signposts here...turn left along the tarmac path following cycle way 14. This path is part of the Derwent Walk.

Follow the Derwent walk for about 1 ½ miles. Keep following the cycle way 14 sign and you will pass the Armstrong factory on your left. Continue along the Derwent walk/cycleway 14, go through a gate onto an open grass area with Fawcett Park circular memorial place showing scenes of the steelworks immediately in front of you.

Cross straight through this and continue to follow the path with the houses on your left. You will cross two roads and when you come to a left turn marked Derwent walk/ cycle way (7). Turn left and this leads to the junction with the Waskerly Way. Turn right along the Waskerly Way with the slag wagon behind you.

Follow this track across the Hownsgill viaduct. Immediately past the viaduct turn right to a footpath through some trees with a fence at your right to a stile. Cross the stile into a field and head straight on with the fence and escarpment on your right.

Follow this for about 400 yards. You will see a stile in the fence to your right heading down through the escarpment through the trees. Cross the stile and continue down this path which is steep in places.

At the bottom of the path you come to a field, cross it diagonally to the left across a small planked bridge and up a small slope through some trees keeping to the right of the houses. As you pass by the rear of the houses you emerge at the top of some steps, walk down them and turn left along the path and at the main road turn left passing the Castleside sign. Walk along the road for about 400 yards and just past the Horse and Groom pub cross the road to a public footpath sign next to a bus stop.

Follow this path downhill and as it opens up it reveals lovely views down the valley to Shotley Bridge. Ignore 3 paths off to the left into the Woodland Trust area. At a fork in the path bear left and then straight on taking the path downhill following the path of the overhead power lines.

As you head downhill you will eventually come to another junction with several paths off it. Take the second path on the right through stone blocks at the entrance and onto an enclosed path. After about 100 yards turn left at a public footpath sign crossing over a stile and walk straight downhill passing through two metal kissing gates of a Woodland Trust area until you come to a main road.

Cross the road and walk through the hedge into Allensford Park. Turn left and head towards the house in the distance, bear right past it onto the bridge on the A68. Turn right across the bridge. Immediately after the house on your right, turn right and then bear left up a small pathway next to the wall onto a public footpath signposted Shotley Bridge 1¾ miles.

In about 300 yards there is a track to your right which leads down to the Allensford Steel Furnace if you wish to visit.

Continue along the main path and at the end of the fence go downhill towards the river and continue along this path next to the river until you come to a bridge across the river at Shotley Bridge. Cross the bridge through the carpark and turn left up the tarmac road. In about 200 yards at a junction, turn immediately right up the hill following the road and 50 yards after some houses on your left take the public footpath on your right and follow this path to a road in about half a mile.

At the road turn right and continue for about 200 metres crossing the road to a disused gated car park. Head to the right hand corner across a small planked bridge to some steps. Follow these steps up to the top of the hill. A steep climb. Turn left at the top and follow the track as it bears right towards the Fawcett Park Memorial place. Turn left here retracing your steps back down the Derwent walk to come to the grassed area where you turn right up St Aidans Street and back to the Lodge in the park.

Refreshments

Hownsgill Tea Rooms, Hownsgill Farm, Consett, County Durham DH8 9AA
Tel. 01207 503597. Open every day except Tuesdays 9.00am – 4.00pm.
Cafe at Inn on The Park at Allensford Park, Pemberton Road, Allensford DH8 9BA
Tel. 01207 513169. Mon - Sun 10am-5pm.
Horse and Groom, Consett road, Castleside DH8 9QQ Tel. 01207 438955

Consett

The Consett Iron Company was established in 1864, a successor of the original Derwent Iron Company of 1840, when the first blast furnaces were introduced. Over the next 100 years, Consett became one of the world's most prominent steel making towns. And the name Consett became synonymous with iron and steel, making the steel for Blackpool Tower and Britain's most famous nuclear submarines. Steel dominated Consett's economy for 140 years. The steelworks was visually spectacular too. And the town was renowned for images of its tall cooling towers and other large plant looming over rows of terraced houses. The towns people could hear the ghostly sounds of the works through the night. During the iron and steel era, a pall of red dust hung over the town: airborne iron oxide from the steel making plant. At its peak in the 1960's, Consett steel works employed 6000 workers and was nationalised to become part of the large British Steel Corporation.

Although there was intense competition in the 1970's from both British competitors and from abroad, Consett steelworks remained relatively successful and was making a profit in the year that it was closed. As the rolling mills were closed in 1970's, despite local opposition, there were rumours and heated discussions over the future of the plant as a whole.

Consett steelworks had always avoided closure, even in difficult times, but in 1980 it was closed with the loss of 4300 jobs plus many more from the knock on effect in ancillary industries. It was a devastating blow. The unemployment rate in Consett doubled the national average.

The steelworks were demolished creating a massive hole in the centre of the town- 700 acres of derelict land. So it was from this the genesis project started a new beginning for Consett.

Hownsgill viaduct

The Stockton & Darlington Railway proposed to build a bridge at Hownes Gill and they commissioned Thomas Bouch to design and supervise its construction. Bouch's design was submitted to Robert Stephenson, who recommended the use of inverted arches under the five central piers to reduce ground loading.

John Anderson started works in 1857 with three million white firebricks being used in the structure, with sandstone Ashlar dressings, and iron railings along the platform. The completed single-track bridge opened in 1858, 700 feet (210 m) long and at maximum 150 feet (46 m) high, spanned by twelve 50 feet (15 m) wide arches on slender triple-tiered piers, with arched recesses in three layers on each side.

The railway line was fully closed in the early 1980s, with the tracks lifted by 1985. The bridge is now part of the Sustrans national foot and cycle path network as part of the Sea to Sea Cycle Route, which crosses from Whitehaven/Workington on the west coast to Sunderland/Tynemouth on the east coast. In 2013 anti-suicide fences were fitted to the bridge; there was one suicide from the bridge every two weeks in the first half of 2011 and five between January and August 2012. (Wikipedia)

Allensford Steel furnace

The blast furnace was used around 1700 and is the earliest surviving ore roasting furnace in Britain; once extracted the iron was sent to a steel forge further downstream which supplied the Shotley Bridge sword makers.

Shotley Bridge

The village has historical origins of swordmaking here dated from 1691. A group of Lutheran swordmakers from Solingen in Germany settled in Shotley Bridge, allegedly in order to escape religious persecution, though in practice their departure was prompted by their breaking of guild oaths. Shotley Bridge was probably chosen because of the rich iron deposits in the area and because of the fast flowing waters of the River Derwent, providing hydraulic power for hammers and grinders. Another factor may have been the remoteness of the area, as the swordmakers were keen to preserve their trade secrets, those that they had illegally taken with them from Germany. The swordmakers were able to employ the services of the famous local engraver Thomas Bewick. Swords are no longer made in the Shotley Bridge district. (Wikipaedia)

Blackhill and Consett Park

The park was created on land gifted to the town by the Consett Iron Company, opening in 1891, to provide a green space where local people could relax, enjoy recreation and exercise in a beautiful parkland setting. The park also provides a well-used pedestrian link between Blackhill and Consett.

In 2002, the park underwent a substantial refurbishment. The park contains a number of interesting features, including a Victorian style bandstand, an outdoor theatre space, a traditional drinking fountain known as Little Edwards and The Wishing Stone where you can make a wish.

In 2009 the former park keepers house was modernised and converted into a public facility to support the various activities and events – The Lodge. It also provides a base for the Consett & District Heritage Initiative, a community history group who hold regular exhibitions, talks, maintain a huge digital archive of old photographs and other materials. The community garden is located behind The Lodge and provides a space where individuals and groups can learn the basics of vegetable growing and other practical gardening skills, in a supportive environment. The Lodge now serves as one of three heritage and visitor information centres for the Land of oak and iron.

Castle Hill wood in Castleside

Castle Hill consists of native broadleaf trees and shrubs. Part of the wood contains an old quarry now dominated by gorse scrubland that provides valuable wildlife habitats including pools and boggy areas.

Notes